W9-BDY-838

The Rubaiyat of Omar Khayyam

Rendered into English Verse

BY EDWARD FITZGERALD

Designed by
Scharr
Design

PETER PAUPER PRESS, INC.
WHITE PLAINS · NEW YORK

*O*mar Khayyam, a scientist as well as a poet, lived in Persia 900 years ago; he was born in the second half of the eleventh century, and died in 1123. Although his name means Omar the Tentmaker (probably after his father's profession) and we think of him only as a pleasure-seeking poet, he was actually best known in his own day as a mathematician and astronomer. He was, in fact, the leading mathematician of his time, author of an algebra which was translated into English as late as 1850, author of other learned works, and member of a commission which reformed the Persian calendar. But today we have forgotten these scientific works and remember him only for his **Rubaiyat**, or epigrammatic quatrains. These quatrains were first noticed in our Western world about 1700, but were not popular until Edward Fitzgerald published his translation of them in 1859—or, rather, until that at-first-neglected anonymous publication was given notoriety by Rossetti's enthusiasm in 1860. Part of the secret of that enthusiasm, and of the poem's present popularity, is that while the original quatrains of Omar were separate epigrams, Fitzgerald, keeping their original stanza form, wove them into a connected poem. The present edition follows Fitzgerald's fourth edition text, incorporating many changes and additions.

THE RUBAIYAT

OF OMAR KHAYYAM

1

*W*ake! For the Sun, who scatter'd into flight
The Stars before him from the Field of Night,
Drives Night along with them from Heav'n,
    and strikes
The Sultán's Turret with a Shaft of Light.

2

Before the Phantom of false Morning died,
Methought a Voice within the Tavern cried,
"When all the Temple is prepar'd within,
Why nods the drowsy Worshiper outside?"

3

And, as the Cock crew, those who stood before
The Tavern shouted—"Open then the Door!
You know how little while we have to stay,
And, once departed, may return no more."

4

Now the New Year reviving old Desires,
The thoughtful Soul to Solitude retires,
Where the white hand of Moses on the Bough
Puts out, and Jesus from the ground suspires.

5

Iram indeed is gone with all its Rose
And Jamshyd's Seven-ring'd Cup where no
  one knows;
But still a Ruby kindles in the Vine,
And many a Garden by the Water blows.

6

And David's Lips are lockt; but in divine
High-piping Pehlevi, with "Wine! Wine!
    Wine!
Red Wine!"—the Nightingale cries to the
    Rose
That sallow Cheek of hers to'incarnadine.

7

Come, fill the Cup, and in the Fire of Spring
Your Winter-garment of Repentance fling:
The Bird of Time has but a little way
To flutter—and the Bird is on the Wing.

8

Whether at Naishápúr or Babylon,
Whether the Cup with sweet or bitter run,
The Wine of Life keeps oozing drop by drop,
The leaves of Life keep falling one by one.

9

Each Morn a thousand Roses brings, you say;
Yes, but where leaves the Rose of Yesterday?
And this first Summer month that brings the
  Rose
Shall take Jamshyd and Kaikobád away.

10

*Well, let it take them! What have we to do
With Kaikobád the Great, or Kaikhosrú?
Let Zál and Rustum bluster as they will,
Or Hátim call to Supper—heed not you.*

11

*With me along the strip of Herbage strown
That just divides the desert from the sown,
Where name of Slave and Sultán is forgot—
And peace to Mahmúd on his golden Throne!*

12

A Book of Verses underneath the Bough,
A Jug of Wine, a Loaf of Bread—and Thou
Beside me singing in the Wilderness—
Oh, Wilderness were Paradise enow!

13

Some for the Glories of This World; and some
Sigh for the Prophet's Paradise to come;
Ah, take the Cash, and let the Credit go,
Nor heed the rumble of a distant Drum!

14

Look to the blowing Rose about us—"Lo,
Laughing," she says, "into the World I blow,
At once the silken Tassel of my Purse
Tear, and its Treasure on the Garden throw."

15

And those who husbanded the Golden Grain,
And those who flung it to the Winds like rain,
Alike to no such aureate Earth are turn'd
As, buried once, Men want dug up again.

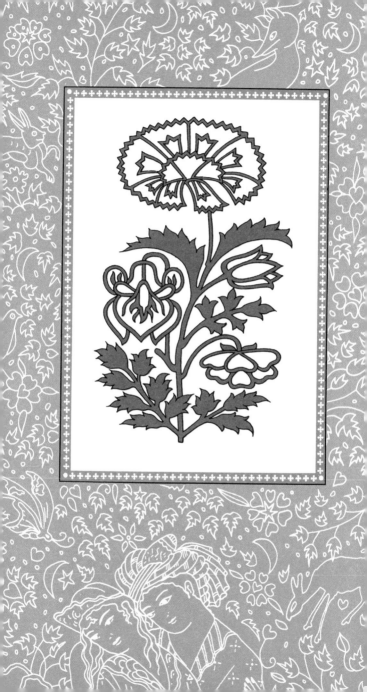

16

The Worldly Hope men set their Hearts upon
Turns Ashes—or it prospers; and anon,
Like Snow upon the Desert's dusty Face
Lighting a little Hour or two—is gone.

17

Think, in this batter'd Caravanserai
Whose Portals are alternate Night and Day,
How Sultán after Sultán with his Pomp
Abode his destin'd Hour, and went his way.

18

They say the Lion and the Lizard keep
The Courts where Jamshyd gloried and drank
*   deep;*
And Bahrám, that great hunter—the wild Ass
Stamps o'er his Head, but cannot break his
*   Sleep.*

19

I sometimes think that never blows so red
The Rose as where some buried Caesar bled;
That every Hyacinth the Garden wears
Dropt in her Lap from some once lovely Head.

20

*And this reviving Herb whose tender Green
Fledges the River-Lip on which we lean—
Ah, lean upon it lightly; for who knows
From what once lovely Lip it springs unseen!*

21

*Ah, my Belovéd, fill the Cup that clears
To-day of past Regrets and future Fears—
To-morrow?—Why, To-morrow I may be
Myself with Yesterday's Sev'n Thousand
Years.*

22

For some we lov'd, the loveliest and the best
That from his Vintage rolling Time hath
*   prest,*
Have drunk their Cup a Round or two before,
And one by one crept silently to Rest.

23

And we, that now make merry in the Room
They left, and Summer dresses in new Bloom,
Ourselves must we beneath the Couch of Earth
Descend ourselves to make a couch—for whom?

24

Ah, make the most of what we yet may spend,
Before we too into the Dust descend;
Dust into Dust, and under Dust, to lie,
Sans Wine, sans Song, sans Singer and—
sans End!

25

Alike for those who for To-day prepare,
And those that after some To-morrow stare,
A Muezzin from the Tower of Darkness cries
"Fools! your Reward is neither Here nor
There!"

26

Why, all the Saints and Sages who discuss'd
Of the Two Worlds so wisely—they are thrust
Like foolish Prophets forth; their words to scorn
  Are scatter'd, and their Mouths are stopt with
     Dust.

27

Myself when young did eagerly frequent
Doctor and Saint, and heard great Argument
About it and about: but evermore
  Came out by the same Door where in I went.

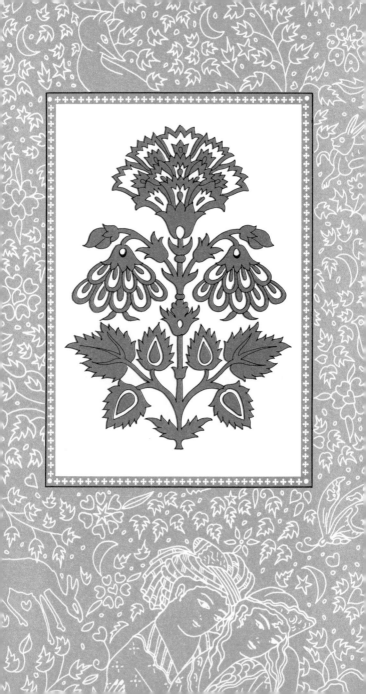

28

With them the Seed of Wisdom did I sow,
And with mine own Hand wrought to make
*   it grow*
And this was all the Harvest that I reap'd—
"I came like Water, and like Wind I go."

29

Into this Universe, and Why not knowing,
Nor Whence, like Water willy-nilly flowing:
And out of it, as Wind along the Waste,
I know not Whither, willy-nilly blowing.

30

What, without asking, hither hurried Whence?
And, without asking, Whither hurried hence!
Oh, many a Cup of this forbidden Wine
Must drown the Memory of that Insolence!

31

Up from Earth's Centre through the Seventh
  Gate
I rose, and on the Throne of Saturn sate,
And many a Knot unravell'd by the Road;
But not the Master-knot of Human Fate.

32

There was the Door to which I found no Key;
There was the Veil through which I might not
    see:
Some little Talk awhile of Me and Thee
There was—and then no more of Thee and Me.

33

Earth could not answer; nor the Seas that
    mourn
In flowing Purple, of their Lord forlorn;
Nor rolling heaven, with all his signs reveal'd
And hidden by the Sleeve of Night and Morn.

34

Then of the Thee in Me who works behind
The Veil, I lifted up my Hands to find
A Lamp amid the Darkness; and I heard,
As from Without— "The Me within Thee
    blind!"

35

Then to the Lip of this poor earthen Urn
I lean'd, the Secret of my Life to learn:
And Lip to Lip it murmur'd— "While you
    live
Drink!—for once dead you never shall return."

36

I think the Vessel, that with fugitive
Articulation answer'd, once did live,
And drink; and Ah! the passive Lip I kiss'd,
How many Kisses might it take—and give!

37

For I remember stopping by the Way
To watch a Potter thumping his wet Clay:
And with its all-obliterated Tongue
It murmur'd— "Gently, Brother, gently,
*   pray!"*

38

And has not such a Story from of Old
Down Man's successive Generations roll'd
Of such a Clod of saturated Earth
Cast by the Maker into Human mould?

39

And not a drop that from our Cups we throw
For Earth to drink of, but may steal below
To quench the fire of Anguish in some Eye
There hidden—far beneath, and long ago.

40

As then the Tulip for her morning Sup
Of Heav'nly Vintage from the soil looks up,
Do you devoutly do the like, till Heav'n
To Earth invert you—like an empty Cup.

41

Perplext no more with Human or Divine,
To-morrow's Tangle to the winds resign,
And lose your Fingers in the tresses of
The Cypress-slender Minister of Wine.

42

And if the Wine you drink, the Lip you press,
End in what All begins and ends in—Yes;
Think then you are To-day what Yesterday
You were—To-morrow you shall not be less.

43

So when that Angel of the darker Drink
At last shall find you by the River-brink,
And, offering his Cup, invite your Soul
Forth to your Lips to quaff—you shall not
*   shrink.*

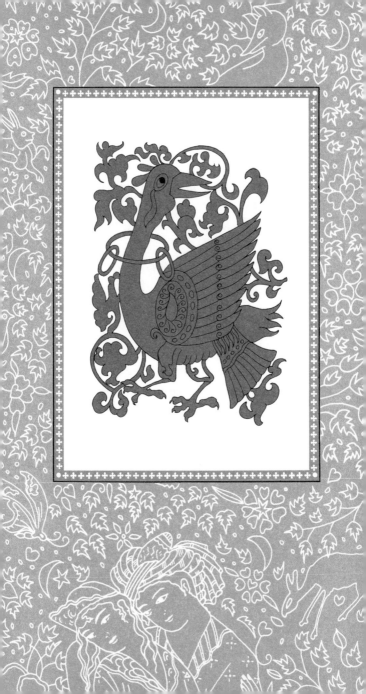

44

Why, if the Soul can fling the Dust aside,
And naked on the Air of Heaven ride,
Were't not a Shame—were't not a Shame
    for him
In this clay carcase crippl'd to abide?

45

'Tis but a Tent where takes his one day's rest
A Sultán to the Realm of Death addrest;
The Sultán rises, and the dark Ferrásh
Strikes, and prepares it for another Guest.

46

And fear not lest Existence closing your
Account, and mine, should know the like no
*   more;*
The Eternal Sáki from that Bowl has pour'd
Millions of Bubbles like us, and will pour.

47

When You and I behind the Veil are past,
Oh, but the long, long while the World shall
*   last,*
Which of our Coming and Departure heeds
As the sea's self should heed a Pebble-cast.

48

A Moment's Halt—a momentary Taste
Of Being from the Well amid the Waste—
And Lo!—the phantom Caravan has reach'd
The Nothing it set out from—Oh, make
*   haste!*

49

Would you that spangle of Existence spend
About the secret—quick about it, Friend!
A Hair perhaps divides the False and True—
And upon what, prithee, may Life depend?

50

A Hair perhaps divides the False and True;
Yes; and a single Alif were the Clue—
Could you but find it—to the Treasure-house,
And peradventure to The Master too;

51

Whose secret Presence, through Creation's
*   veins*
Running Quicksilver-like eludes your pains;
Taking all shapes from Máh to Máhi; and
They change and perish all—but He remains;

52

A moment guess'd—then back behind the fold
Immerst of Darkness round the Drama roll'd
Which, for the Pastime of Eternity,
He doth Himself contrive, enact, behold.

53

But if in vain, down on the stubborn Floor
Of earth, and up to Heav'n's unopening door,
You gaze To-day, while You are You—how
*   then*
To-morrow, when You shall be You no more?

54

Waste not your Hour, nor in the vain pursuit
Of This and That endeavour and dispute;
Better be jocund with the fruitful Grape
Than sadden after none, or bitter, Fruit.

55

You know, my Friends, with what a brave
*   Carouse*
I made a Second Marriage in my House;
Divorc'd old barren Reason from my Bed,
And took the Daughter of the Vine to Spouse.

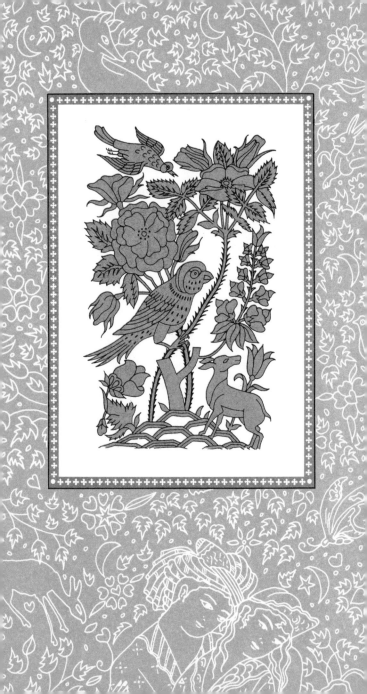

56

For "Is" and "Is-not" though with Rule and Line
And "Up-and-down" by Logic I define,
Of all that one should care to fathom, I
Was never deep in anything but—Wine.

57

Ah, but my Computations, People say,
Reduc'd the Year to better reckoning?—Nay,
'Twas only striking from the Calendar
Unborn To-morrow, and dead Yesterday.

58

And lately, by the Tavern Door agape,
Came shining through the Dusk an Angel
*   Shape*
Bearing a Vessel on his Shoulder; and
He bid me taste of it; and 'twas — the Grape!

59

The Grape that can with Logic absolute
The Two-and-Seventy jarring Sects confute:
The sovereign Alchemist that in a trice
Life's leaden Metal into Gold transmute;

60

The mighty Mahmúd, Allah-breathing Lord,
That all the misbelieving and black Horde
Of Fears and Sorrows that infest the Soul
Scatters before him with his whirlwind Sword.

61

Why, be this Juice the growth of God, who dare
Blaspheme the twisted Tendril as a Snare?
A Blessing, we should use it, should we not?
And if a Curse—why, then, Who set it there?

62

I must abjure the Balm of Life, I must,
Scar'd by some After-reckoning ta'en on trust,
Or lur'd with Hope of some diviner Drink,
To fill the Cup—when crumbl'd into Dust!

63

Oh threats of Hell and Hopes of Paradise!
One thing at least is certain—this Life flies;
One thing is certain and the rest is Lies;
The Flower that once has blown for ever dies.

64

Strange, is it not? that of the Myriads who
Before us pass'd the door of Darkness through,
Not one returns to tell us of the Road,
Which to discover we must travel too.

65

The Revelations of Devout and Learn'd
Who rose before us, and as Prophets burn'd,
Are all but Stories, which, awoke from Sleep
They told their comrades, and to Sleep return'd.

66

I sent my Soul through the Invisible,
Some Letter of that After-Life to spell:
And by and by my Soul return'd to me,
And answer'd "I Myself am Heav'n and
    Hell."

67

Heav'n but the Vision of fulfill'd Desire,
And Hell the Shadow from a Soul on fire,
Cast on the Darkness into which Ourselves,
So late emerg'd from, shall so soon expire.

68

We are no other than a moving Row
Of magic Shadow-Shapes that come and go
Round with the Sun-illumin'd Lantern held
In Midnight by the Master of the Show.

69

But helpless Pieces of the Game He plays
Upon this Chequer-board of Nights and Days;
Hither and thither moves, and checks, and
      slays,
And one by one back in the Closet lays.

70

The Ball no question makes of Ayes and Noes;
But Here or There as strikes the Player goes;
And He that toss'd you down into the Field,
He knows about it all—He knows—
　　HE KNOWS!

71

The Moving Finger writes; and, having writ,
Moves on: nor all your Piety nor Wit,
Shall lure it back to cancel half a Line,
Nor all your Tears wash out a Word of it.

72

And that inverted Bowl they call the Sky,
Whereunder crawling coop'd we live and die,
Lift not your Hands to It for help—for It
As impotently moves as you or I.

73

With Earth's first Clay They did the Last
*   Man knead,*
And there of the Last Harvest sow'd the Seed:
And the first Morning of Creation wrote
What the Last Dawn of Reckoning shall read.

74

Yesterday this Day's Madness did prepare;
To-morrow's Silence, Triumph, or Despair:
Drink; for you know not whence you came,
* nor why:*
Drink; for you know not why you go, nor
* where.*

75

I tell you this — When, started from the Goal,
Over the flaming Shoulders of the Foal
Of Heav'n Parwin and Mushtari they flung,
In my predestin'd Plot of Dust and Soul.

76

The Vine had struck a Fibre: which about
If clings my Being—let the Dervish flout;
Of my Base metal may be fil'd a Key
That shall unlock the Door he howls without.

77

And this I know: whether the one True Light
Kindle to Love, or Wrath consume me quite,
One Flash of It within the Tavern caught
Better than in the Temple lost outright.

78

What! out of senseless Nothing to provoke
A conscious Something to resent the Yoke
Of unpermitted Pleasure, under pain
Of Everlasting Penalties, if broke!

79

What! from His helpless Creature be repaid
Pure Gold for what He lent him dross-allay'd:
Sue for a Debt he never did contract,
And cannot answer—Oh the sorry Trade!

80

Oh Thou, who didst with Pitfall and with Gin
Beset the Road I was to wander in,
Thou wilt not with Predestin'd Evil round
Enmesh, and then impute my Fall to Sin!

81

Oh Thou, who Man of baser Earth didst make,
And ev'n with Paradise devise the Snake:
For all the Sin wherewith the Face of Man
Is blacken'd, Man's Forgiveness give—
  and take!

82

As under cover of departing Day
Slunk hunger-stricken Ramazán away
Once more within the Potter's House alone
I stood, surrounded by the Shapes of Clay.

83

Shapes of all Sorts and Sizes, great and small,
That stood along the floor and by the wall;
And some loquacious Vessels were; and some
Listen'd perhaps, but never talk'd at all.

84

Said one among them— "Surely not in vain
My substance of the common Earth was ta'en
And to this Figure moulded, to be broke,
Or trampl'd back to shapeless Earth again."

85

Then said a Second— "Ne'er a peevish Boy
Would break the Bowl from which he drank
*   in joy;*
And He that with His hand the Vessel made
Will surely not in after Wrath destroy."

86

After a momentary Silence spake
Some Vessel of a more ungainly Make;
"They sneer at me for leaning all awry;
What! did the Hand then of the Potter shake?"

87

Whereat some one of the loquacious Lot—
I think a Sufi Pipkin—waxing hot—
"All this of Pot and Potter—Tell me then,
Who is the Potter, pray, and who the Pot?"

88

"Why," said another, "Some there are who tell
Of one who threatens he will toss to Hell
The luckless Pots he marr'd in màking—Pish!
He's a Good Fellow, and 'twill all be well."

89

"Well," murmur'd one, "Let whoso make or
  buy,
My Clay with long Oblivion is gone dry:
But, fill me with the old familiar Juice,
Methinks I might recover by and by!"

90

So while the Vessels one by one were speaking,
The little Moon look'd in that all were seeking:
And then they jogg'd each other, "Brother!
    Brother!
Now for the Porter's shoulder knot a-creaking!"

91

Ah, with the Grape my fading Life provide,
And wash the Body whence the Life has died,
And lay me, shrouded in the living Leaf,
By some not unfrequented Garden-side.

92

That ev'n my buried Ashes such a Snare
Of Vintage shall fling up into the Air
As not a True Believer passing by
But shall be overtaken unaware.

93

Indeed the Idols I have lov'd so long
Have done my Credit in this World much
        wrong:
Have drown'd my Glory in a shallow Cup,
And sold my Reputation for a Song.

94

Indeed, indeed, Repentance oft before
I swore—but was I sober when I swore?
And then and then came Spring, and Rose-
*   in-hand*
My threadbare Penitence a-pieces tore.

95

And much as Wine has play'd the Infidel,
And robb'd me of my Robe of Honour—well,
I wonder often what the Vintners buy
One-half so precious as the Stuff they sell.

96

Yet Ah, that Spring should vanish with the
    Rose!
That Youth's sweet-scented Manuscript
    should close!
The Nightingale that in the Branches sang,
Ah, whence, and whither flown again, who
    knows!

97

Would but the Desert of the Mountain yield
One glimpse—if dimly, yet indeed, reveal'd,
To which the fainting Traveller might
    spring,
As springs that trampl'd herbage of the field!

98

Would but some wingéd Angel ere too late
Arrest the yet unfolded Roll of Fate,
And make the stern Recorder otherwise
Enregister, or quite obliterate!

99

Ah Love! could you and I with Him conspire
To grasp this sorry Scheme of Things entire,
Would not we shatter it to bits—and then
Re-mould it nearer to the Heart's Desire!

100

Yon rising Moon that looks for us again—
How oft hereafter will she wax and wane;
How oft hereafter rising look for us
Through this same Garden—and for one in
vain!

101

And when like her, oh Sáki, you shall pass
Among the Guests Star-scatter'd on the Grass,
And in your joyous Errand reach the Spot
Where I made One—turn down an empty
Glass!